THE WHITE HOUSE

BY M. WEBER

Published by The Child's World®
1980 Lookout Drive • Mankato, MN 56003-1705
800-599-READ • www.childsworld.com

ISBN 9781503845008 (REINFORCED LIBRARY BINDING)
ISBN 9781503846364 (PORTABLE DOCUMENT FORMAT)
ISBN 9781503847552 (ONLINE MULTI-USER EBOOK)
LCCN: 2019956631

Printed in the United States of America

**On the cover: The White House is one of the
most recognizable buildings in the United States.**

TABLE OF CONTENTS

CHAPTER 1

BUILDING THE WHITE HOUSE

The White House is where the president of the United States lives. The president also works there. The White House is in Washington, DC. Today, it is well known. But when the United States was founded, it was not built yet. The Founding Fathers had to decide where the **capital city** would be. This is also where the president would live. The Founding Fathers were men who helped create the United States. They wrote the Constitution. They created the three **branches of government**. They also had to decide on a capital city. The president would live in the capital.

The Founding Fathers could not agree on where the capital should be. America was still a new country. There were only 13 states. Philadelphia was an important city. So was New York City. Some thought the capital should be in one of those two cities. Instead, the Founding Fathers decided to build a brand-new city.

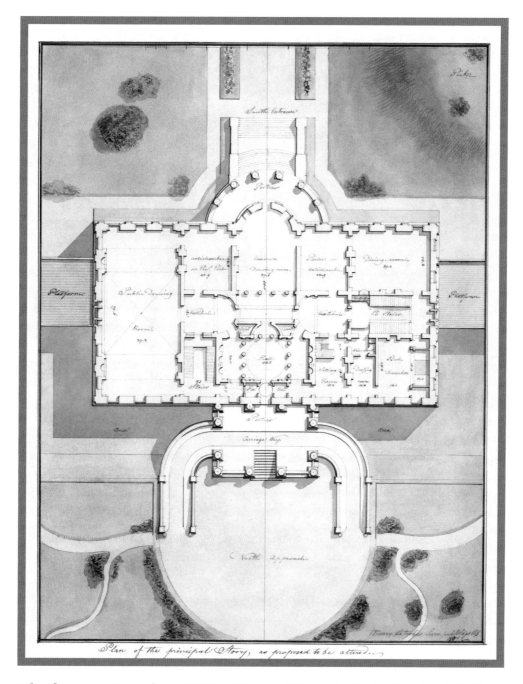

The first version of the White House did not include the Oval Office.

**When the Capitol Building was built, it was
surrounded by fields and forests.**

George Washington wanted the city to be on the
Potomac River. Two states touched the river. Maryland and
Virginia agreed to donate, or give, the land for the capital.
The city would not belong to either state. It would be a
separate **district**. Washington, District of Columbia, was
founded in July 1790. Now the city is called Washington,
DC. America's national government, which includes the
president, is based there.

MAN OF MANY TALENTS

Thomas Jefferson submitted a proposal to the White House contest. He also drew plans for his own home. It is called Monticello. Jefferson designed buildings at the University of Virginia. Today, a type of architecture is named after him. It is called Jeffersonian architecture.

The Constitution gave the Founding Fathers the right to build a capital city. There were only small settlements in the area before it became the capital. Pierre Charles L'Enfant was chosen to design the city. He knew it would be the capital. He also knew the president would live there. He decided to put the White House on a hill. It was at one end of the city. At the other end of the city is the **Capitol Building**. It is also on a hill. This shows the importance of both buildings.

Thomas Jefferson suggested holding a contest. The winner of the contest would get to design the White House. Many people could submit designs. People from around the country entered the contest. The winner was an architect from Philadelphia named James Hoban. An architect is someone who designs buildings. Washington helped finish the design. Washington lived in Philadelphia and New York City. He directed the building of the White House from those places.

People in Washington, DC, still boat and fish on the Potomac River.

Construction began on October 13, 1792. It took eight years. The White House was built with sandstone. This special kind of rock came from Virginia. It is only found near Aquia Creek. The gray and white color of the stone made the building stand out. The other buildings around it were mostly made of brick. It was built by hired workers. Slaves also worked on it. Both workers and slaves lived in temporary huts on the grounds of the White House. At first the building was called the Executive Mansion. People started calling it the White House because of the color. The White House became the official name in 1901.

CHAPTER 2

EARLY YEARS OF THE WHITE HOUSE

George Washington did not live to see the completion of the White House. He died in 1799. The White House was finished in 1800. The first president to live in the White House was John Adams. His wife was Abigail Adams. They moved into the house in November 1800. Construction had finished on the White House. However, many rooms were incomplete. It was also cold in the White House. It was heated by fireplaces. The rooms were large. It took large fires to stay warm. John and Abigail Adams lived there for four months. Then a new president was elected. Thomas Jefferson was the third president of the United States. He moved into the White House on March 4, 1801. This was also the day he was inaugurated as president.

HAVE YOU ANY WOOL?

Woodrow Wilson was president from 1913 to 1921. This was during World War I (1914–1918). President Wilson kept sheep on the lawn of the White House. It saved money on lawn maintenance. He sold the wool to raise money for the **Red Cross**.

Dolley Madison risked her life to save a
portrait of George Washington from a fire.
It destroyed the White House in 1814.

Thomas Jefferson was the first president to make
big changes to the White House. He hired a man named
Benjamin Henry Latrobe. Jefferson put Latrobe in charge
of all public buildings in the city in 1803. It was also his job
to make the White House better. Latrobe fixed a leaking
roof. He created a new grand staircase. He also moved the
main entrance to the north side of the White House. This
is still the main entrance. Jefferson was also responsible
for the lawns. He planted new trees. He planted flowers.
Jefferson wanted to build a garden wall. All of these
changes added to the outside of the White House. Inside,
he turned a dining room into his office. He decorated rooms
with wallpaper he ordered from France.

James Madison followed Thomas Jefferson as president.
There was a war during his presidency. The United States
went to war against England. This is known as the War of
1812 (1812–1815). Madison's wife was Dolley Madison.
They lived in the White House together. British troops
threatened the White House. The president and his wife
had to flee. A large portrait of George Washington hung in
the White House. It was eight feet tall and hard to move.

President William Howard Taft's Oval Office rug was dark green. Each president changes the room's colors when they take office.

Dolley Madison refused to leave the White House without it. The British army burned the White House on August 24, 1814. But the president and his wife were safe. So was the portrait of the first President. It hangs in the White House today.

President Theodore Roosevelt made major updates to the White House in 1902. He had the West Wing built. The West Wing is home to the president's offices. His staff also works in the West Wing. The Oval Office is in the West Wing. It was added by President William Howard Taft. This is the president's main office. Every president since 1909 has worked in the Oval Office.

CHAPTER 3

CHANGES TO THE WHITE HOUSE

Each president can make changes to the White House. Presidents can change decorations. They can also change carpet and drapes. Presidents have different preferences. The president's family should feel at home in the White House. The **first family** lives on the second floor. This is the **residential** wing. The president's spouse is usually in charge of decorating this area. It is harder to change the public rooms of the White House. All changes must be approved. The Committee for the Preservation of the White House gives approval.

There are some traditions for White House decorations. Presidents can choose the paintings that hang in the Oval Office. Most presidents choose to display portraits of their favorite **predecessors**.

I DO!

There have been 18 weddings held at the White House. Often the weddings are for members of the president's family. But one wedding was for a president! President Grover Cleveland married Frances Folsom in 1886 while in office. They were married in the Blue Room.

Each Oval Office rug includes the Presidential Seal, but colors and other designs on the rug change with each new president.

The president or his or her spouse can also design the rug. The rug in the Oval Office usually includes the presidential seal. The desk in the Oval Office is called the Resolute Desk. It is made from wood taken from a ship called HMS *Resolute*. Rutherford B. Hayes was the first president to use the desk. It has been used by all but three presidents since 1879.

John F. Kennedy took office in 1961. His wife was Jacqueline Kennedy. Mrs. Kennedy helped restore many rooms in the White House. Many important **artifacts** are kept in the White House. Mrs. Kennedy felt that the artifacts belonged to the American people. She led a tour that was shown on television. The Kennedys helped make the White House an official museum. They wanted to make sure the artwork and artifacts inside were protected by the government.

Over time, the White House has changed on the inside and outside. Electricity was installed in 1891. A large circular driveway was completed in 1970. Official visitors to the White House use the driveway. A press briefing room was also added inside the White House. This is where the president can speak to reporters. Some updates also keep the White House modern. The first computers were installed by President Jimmy Carter in 1978.

The White House is the president's home and office. But it also hosts many events. Many are long-standing traditions. One is the Easter Egg Roll. It started in 1878. The event happens on Easter Monday. Children and families are invited to the White House.

There are 320 place settings in the official White House china service. This means a state dinner can host 320 people.

There are games on the White House lawn. Every first family can make changes to the event. This way it feels special to each president.

The president also uses the White House for official business. State dinners are held at the White House. A state dinner is when the president welcomes the leader of another country. The first state dinner was held by Ulysses S. Grant in 1874. He welcomed the king of Hawaii. Hawaii was not yet an American state. This is how the White House serves as both home and office to the president.

CHAPTER 4

THE WHITE HOUSE TODAY

Today, the White House is still the home and office of the president and first family. Each new president moves into the White House on the afternoon of inauguration day. Every president must find a balance between tradition and modern advances. President George H.W. Bush brought the internet to the White House. It was installed in 1992. It was used for email. The first White House website was created in 1994. Bill Clinton was president at that time. The White House must change as technology changes.

The area around the White House has also changed. The address of the White House is 1600 Pennsylvania Avenue. For a long time, this street was open to all traffic. Part of the street was closed in 1995. Cars and other vehicles are no longer allowed in front of the White House. The street was closed due to safety concerns. However, it is now a popular spot for visitors. People can walk up to the gate and look at the White House. It is also a popular place for people to **protest**.

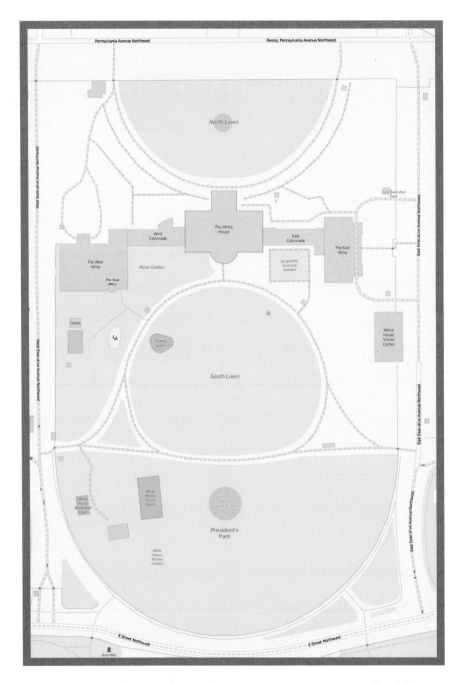

Although it is located in a large city next to many buildings,
the White House is surrounded by a large yard and gardens.

Protest is when people want the attention of the president. They can gather outside the White House.

The White House is sometimes called "the People's House." This means the people of the United States should have access to the White House. However, visiting can be difficult. It is not like a museum. Many people work there. Citizens can contact their representatives in Congress when they want to visit. Their representatives can give them tickets for a tour. Around 1.5 million people visit the White House each year. People can also take a **virtual** tour. In 2013, the White House allowed Google to take 360-degree photos of all public rooms. This means many more people can see inside the People's House.

There are six floors in the White House. This includes below-ground levels. Today, there are a total of 132 rooms. Thirty-five of those rooms are bathrooms. It is a very large building. There are eight staircases and three elevators.

The president sometimes speaks to citizens
and the press from the South Portico.

The White House no longer needs fireplaces for heat. But 28 fireplaces are still used.

The chief usher oversees the White House. The chief usher is in charge of the White House schedule and **budget**. There is a staff of 96 full-time employees. More than 250 part-time employees also work there. The staff does not change when a new president arrives. They often work there for a long time. The staff includes five full-time chefs. The chefs cook for the first family. They also cook for important events. These employees help keep the house running. This allows the president to concentrate on work.

The White House is an important monument for the American people. It reminds them of the history and beliefs of the United States. The White House is both a museum and a symbol of America's future. Although many presidents have lived there, the White House will always be "the People's House."

GLOSSARY

artifacts (AR-ti-fakts) Artifacts are simple objects, such as tools or weapons, or original documents, such as letters or photos, that were created by people in the past.

branches of government (BRAN-chez UHV GUH-vern-ment) The branches of government are the three main parts of the United States government. They include the legislative branch, the executive branch, and the judicial branch.

budget (BUH-jet) A budget is a plan for how a person or organization intends to spend a specific amount of money.

capital city (KA-pi-tul SI-tee) A capital city is the city in a state or country where the government is based.

Capitol Building (KA-pi-tul BILD-ing) The Capitol Building is a domed building in Washington, DC, where the legislative branch of the US government is based.

district (DIS-trikt) A district is an area of a city or country set apart to be used for a particular purpose. The District of Columbia, or Washington, DC, was a section of land in the United States that was separate from surrounding states. It became the capital of the country.

first family (FIRST FA-muh-lee) The first family is the spouse, children, and other immediate family members of the president of the United States or a governor of a US state.

inaugurated (ih-NAH-gyur-ay-ted) When someone is inaugurated, he or she is formally admitted to a public office with a special ceremony.

predecessors (PRED-i-seh-serz) Predecessors are individuals who held a job or position before someone else.

protest (PRO-test) To protest is to show strong disagreement with or disapproval of something. People who protest often gather outside of government buildings and carry signs that express their views.

Red Cross (RED KROSS) The Red Cross is an organization founded to care for sick and wounded people during wars, floods, fires, and other emergency situations.

residential (rez-i-DEN-shul) Residential refers to a part of a building where people live.

virtual (VER-choo-ul) Virtual is something that is not real, but experienced using software created for a computer or other device.

TO LEARN MORE

IN THE LIBRARY

Buchanan, Shelly. *Our Government: The Three Branches.*
Huntington Beach, CA: Teacher Created Materials, 2015.

Mooney, Carla. *The U.S. Constitution: Discover How Democracy Works.* White River Junction, VT: Nomad Press, 2016.

Shamir, Ruby. *What's the Big Deal about Elections.*
New York: Philomel Books, 2018.

ON THE WEB

Visit our website for links to learn more about the White House:

childsworld.com/links

Note to Parents, Teachers, and Librarians: We routinely verify our Web links to make sure they are safe and active sites. So encourage your readers to check them out!

INDEX

ABOUT THE AUTHOR

M. Weber is a teacher and writer. She has written for both kids and adults and enjoys helping people of all ages learn new things. She has written about history, sports, and the environment. When she is not writing, she enjoys spending time with her family and browsing at her local bookstore. She lives in Minnesota.